A Star Will Rise

The Old Testament Roots
of the Magi and Their Journey

A Daily Devotional for Advent

I see him, but not here and now.
I perceive him, but far in the distant future.
A star will rise from Jacob;
a scepter will emerge from Israel.
Numbers 24:17 NLT

Tammy L. Priest
2011

A Star Will Rise: The Old Testament Roots of the Magi and Their Journey
© 2011 Tammy L. Priest
(P. O. Box 25722, Winston-Salem, NC 27114-5722)
ISBN: 978-0-9822526-2-8

Cover Photo © Daevid - Fotolia.com
Cover Design © Tammy L. Priest
Back Cover Photo Credit: Alysia H. Grimes

Scripture Translations

(Used by permission. All rights reserved by copyright holder):

AMP.....................The Amplified Bible (Copyright © 1954, 1958, 1962, 1964, 1965, 1987 by The Lockman Foundation)

ASV......................American Standard Version (public domain)

CEV.....................Contemporary English Version (Copyright © 1995 by the American Bible Society)

Darby ....Darby Translation (Copyright © by J.N. Darby)

DR ....Douay-Rheims (public domain)

ESV......................English Standard Version (Copyright © 2001 by Crossway Bibles, a division of Good News Publishers)

HCSB ....Holman Christian Standard Bible (Copyright © 1999, 2000, 2002, 2003 by Holman Bible Publishers, Nashville, Tennessee)

HNV....................Hebrew Names Version (public domain)

JPS........................Jewish Publication Society (Copyright © 1917, The Jewish Publication Society of America)

KJ21 ....21st Century King James Version (Copyright ©1994 by Deuel Enterprises, Inc., Gary, South Dakota)

KJV ....King James Version (public domain)

The Message.....The Message Translation (Copyright © 2002 by Eugene Peterson)

NAB.....................The New American Bible with Revised New Testament (Copyright © 1986, 1970 Confraternity of Christian Doctrine, Washington, D.C.)

NASB ....New American Standard Bible Copyright © 1960, 1962, 1968, 1971, 1972, 1973, 1975, 1977, 1995 by The Lockman Foundation, La Habra, California)

NCV ....New Century Version (Copyright © 1987, 1988, 1991 by Thomas Nelson, Inc.)

NIRV....................New International Reader's Version (Copyright © 1995, 1996, 1998 by Biblica)

NIV.......................New International Version (Copyright © 1973, 1978, 1984 by Biblica)

NKJV....................New King James Version (Copyright © 1982 by Thomas Nelson, Inc.)

NLT ....New Living Translation (Copyright © 1996, 2004 by Tyndale Charitable Trust)

WNT ....Weymouth New Testament (public domain)

YLT ....Young's Literal Translation (public domain)

For God, who said, "Let light shine out of darkness,"
has shone in our hearts to give the light of the knowledge
of the glory of God in the face of Jesus Christ.

2 Corinthians 4:6 ESV

This devotional is dedicated first and foremost to the Messiah,
whose Light continues to rise in my heart each day
to illuminate my path. And to my husband,
whose partnership in life and love is a priceless gift,
for which I am thankful in every season.

I express a deeply heartfelt thank you to the ladies
of First Baptist Church in Springfield, Virginia. The message they
invited me to share with them in 2007 formed the foundation of
this devotional. In particular, I must thank my treasure of a
mother-in-law, Alison Priest; the tireless Sheri Gay;
and faithful Carol Sikora; women the Lord has used
to greatly bless my heart and my ministry.

I am also thankful for my dear friends,
Deanne Trollinger and Melissa Phipps,
for their honest editing and steadfast encouragement.

"Just over the horizon, a new light is shining.
Salvation's on its way."

(Third Day, © 2010, *Lift Up Your Face*)

Contents

In Your presence, there is fullness of joy...
Psalm 16:11 NASB

"And be sure of this: I am with you always,
even to the end of the age."
Matthew 28:20b NLT

"When you pass through the waters, I will be with you;
and when you pass through the rivers, they will not sweep over you.
When you walk through the fire, you will not be burned;
the flames will not set you ablaze.
For I am the LORD, your God, the Holy One of Israel, your Savior..."
Isaiah 43:2-3 NIV

"Be strong and courageous. Do not be terrified; do not be discouraged,
for the LORD your God will be with you wherever you go."
Joshua 1:9 NIV

God did this so that men would seek him
and perhaps reach out for him and find him, though he is not far from
each one of us. 'For in him we live and move and have our being.'
Acts 17:27-28a NIV

Introduction
What is Advent?

A dvent calendars. Advent wreaths. Advent candles. The official countdown to Christmas is upon us. But what exactly is Advent? Christians first observed this special time of preparation as early as the fourth century. It was a time for new believers to ready their hearts and minds for baptism. Then, over the centuries, the focus of Advent swung back and forth between anticipating the Nativity to awaiting Jesus' second coming.

In reality, all three of these approaches embody what the word "*adventus*" means, and how it should speak to our hearts. At its most *basic* translation, *adventus* means "coming" or "arrival." So we are to spend these days preparing our hearts to celebrate Jesus' humble arrival among us, His transforming Presence within us, and His ultimate triumphant return to us.

But the *full* definition of *adventus* allows us to really grasp the magnitude of what Jesus came to do more than 2,000 years ago, and of what He desires to do in each of us today. *Adventus* is actually the Latin translation of *parousia,* the Greek New Testament word for "arrival" or "presence." It often refers to the arrival or presence of an ordinary person on an ordinary visit. But *parousia* was also used to speak of a king paying a visit, either through a chosen representative, or personally, with a show of great power. And during the first century, *parousia* described the manifestation of a god through acceptable sacrifices.

Applying that full definition, our Magi made their "advent" in Judea, visiting what appeared to be an ordinary baby born to ordinary people. But ordinary He was not. He was the chosen representative of the heavenly King of Kings, arriving on earth to visit mankind. Yet God's messenger did not appear with a flourish of great power, but with the whimper of a babe. He manifested *Himself* in our midst as *Adonai* – God *with* us – in a breathtaking new way. Not in response to any sacrifice we had – or ever could have – made, but in order to make the only truly acceptable sacrifice on our behalf.

The full definition of *parousia* is not merely an arrival, but "includes…the presence which follows the arrival."[1] And that is a perfect, beautiful description of Advent. It is God's decision to come alongside His children in bodily form and remain with us. Not simply for thirty-three years two millennia ago, but to walk with and remain with each one of us *today,* by the indwelling of His Spirit. It is His "being alongside" presence.[2]

So let us celebrate Jesus among us – both then and now – by accompanying the very first people to visit and celebrate His arrival. And as you do, ask the Lord to come along side you, preparing you not only to celebrate His birth, but to accompany you through all that life brings you each day of the journey.

A man's gift makes room for him
and brings him before great men.

Proverbs 18:16 NAS

...The star [the wise men] had seen in the east guided them
to Bethlehem... and stopped over the place where the child was...
they were filled with joy! They entered the house and...bowed down
and worshipped him. Then they opened their treasure chests
and gave him gifts of gold, frankincense and myrrh.

Matthew 2:9-11 NLT

...Every desirable and beneficial gift comes out of heaven.
The gifts are rivers of light cascading down
from the Father of Light...

James 1:17 The Message

For God so greatly loved and dearly prized the world
that He [even] gave up His only begotten ([a]unique) Son,
so that whoever believes in (trusts in, clings to, relies on) Him
shall not perish (come to destruction, be lost)
but have eternal (everlasting) life.

John 3:16 AMP

Day One
The Gift

Welcome to the whirlwind that is December! The Christmas relay race of shopping and shipping, cooking and crafting, and gifting and gathering is now in full swing. For most of us, a change of pace would be nice. So let's slow down together and walk the dusty roads of the desert, coming alongside a caravan of first-century Persians.

Like so many of us, this group of travelers had packed up their presents and were looking forward to a magnificent Christmas celebration. Unlike us, however, this was their very first Christmas gathering, and these were the very first Christmas presents the men – or anyone – had ever given.

❋ Read the verses on the opposite page.

True to Solomon's proverb, the Magi's generous gifts earned them an audience with Jesus, the greatest of all men. But the Magi did not actually initiate the Christmas gift-giving. No, they gave lavishly in response to an even greater present that they had received: God's gift of the Messiah, His own Son, whom He gave to us wrapped in delicate human flesh.

Why did the Almighty send such a priceless gift? A gift so lavish that it is still nearly impossible to fathom. He sent His own Son, a part of His very Being, to enter our world so that He – the King of all Kings – could gain an audience. Not just with "great" men, but with any man, woman or child who will make room for Him in his or her heart and mind. And for no other reason than the simple, yet astounding, fact that He deeply loves and prizes each one of us.

As we approach Christmas and all that it should mean, let us stow away with the Magi, joining our hearts and minds to theirs. For their journey paints a vibrant and sweeping picture of all that Jesus came to give two millennia ago, and of all that He came to give each one of us today.

What Christmas present do you most want to receive this year?
Is it a material gift – a gadget, some jewelry or getaway? Is it something more serious – a healed body, a new job or a restored relationship?
Pray that during this time of Advent, the Lord will speak to your heart about the gift He most wants to give you: Himself.
Pray about what that would look like in your life, and how it might impact your view of all the other gifts – or lack of them – around you.

...excitement was produced in Jerusalem by the arrival
of certain Magi from the east...
Matthew 2:1 WNT

...Assyria deported Israel...and settled them...in towns of the Medes.
2 Kings 18:11 NIV

Mordecai... sent letters to all the Jews throughout the provinces of King
Xerxes...to have them celebrate annually... the time when the Jews got
relief from their enemies. And...a full account of the greatness of
Mordecai...are they not written in the book of the annals of the kings of
Media and Persia? Mordecai the Jew was second in rank to King Xerxes.
Esther 9:20-21, 10:2-3a NIV

Then King Nebuchadnezzar leaped to his feet in amazement
and asked his advisers, "Weren't there three men that we tied up and
threw into the fire?" They replied, "Certainly, O king."
He said, "Look! I see four men walking around in the fire, unbound and
unharmed, and the fourth looks like a son of the gods...
Praise be to the God of Shadrach, Meshach and Abednego...
...no other god can save..."
Daniel 3:24-25, 28-29 NIV

"I kept looking in the night visions, And behold, with the clouds of heaven
One like a Son of Man was coming...And to Him was given dominion,
glory and a kingdom, That all the peoples, nations and men of every
language might serve Him. His dominion is an everlasting dominion which
will not pass away..."

Daniel 7:13-14 NASB

Day Two
Men of the East

T ales of our traveling companions fill Christmas cards and manger scenes. Yet Matthew doesn't really tell us anything about them. He doesn't explain why these "wise men," or "magi" or "kings of the orient" (depending on your translation) came to worship Israel's yet unknown, newborn king.

Perhaps the disciple didn't explain because everyone already knew. First century Jews and Gentiles alike knew that the Magi were a tribe within the Medes with special status, like the Levites within Israel. They practiced astrology, medicine and oriental science, serving as royal advisors on both religious and political matters.[3] The Magi were men with position and power.

Yet the Magi's people had also been through hard times. Six centuries before Jesus' birth, while Babylon was busy carrying Israel into exile, Persia conquered the Medes, folding them into their empire. Then Persia – with Darius the Mede at the helm[4] – turned around and conquered mighty Babylon. The merging of these two empires produced a melting pot of biblical cultures: Persians, Babylonians, Jews, and Medes.

❋ Read the verses on the opposite page. Consider how these events may have impacted the first century Magi.

Think of all that played out in the history of God's people during those times in Persia and Babylon: the drama of Esther, the furnace of fire, the den of lions, and the visions of Daniel. The Medes and their Magi witnessed it all. Yes, those were years of painful exile and enemy overlords for both the Jews and the Medes. But God was weaving it all together in His perfect timing according to His perfect plan.

The Magi knew exactly who the God of Israel was because of everything they had seen and heard. They knew that when God's Anointed finally did arrive, He would not be for the Jews alone, but for all nations and all people – including them. And so, our first-century, gift-bearing Magi set off on their famous journey filled with great expectations. They would not be disappointed.

Your life story is unique. It is probably filled with seasons of both happiness and heartache. Trust that God knows what He is working out in your circumstances and in your heart, and ask Him to reveal Himself to you in a personal and powerful way through it all.

After Jesus was born in Bethlehem of Judea in the days of King Herod,
wise men from the east arrived unexpectedly in Jerusalem, saying,
"Where is He who has been born King of the Jews?
For we saw His star in the east and have come to worship Him."

Matthew 2:1-2 HCSB

"Come and see..."

John 1:39 NLT

"Come, follow me..."

John 1:43 NLT

"Come and see a man...Could he possibly be the Messiah?"
John 4:29 NLT

I saw that the Lamb opened one of the seven seals, and I heard one
of the four living creatures saying, as with a voice of thunder, "Come and
see!" ...the second...saying... "Come!" ...the third...saying, "Come and
see!" ...the fourth...saying, "Come and see!" ...After these things I saw,
and behold, a great multitude, which no man could number, out of every
nation and of all tribes, peoples, and languages, standing before the
throne and before the Lamb...They cried with a loud voice, saying
"Salvation be to our God, who sits on the throne, and to the Lamb."

Revelation 6:1-7, 7:9-10 HNV

Day Three
The Journey Begins

C ome." It was Jesus' simple, repeated invitation to His first disciples. "Come," He called, "follow me." But before Jesus called the twelve, before He could even pronounce the words to call them, a group of men did come. They came across an entire continent, drawn to the One who had come from heaven.

✵ Read the verses on the opposite page. Consider what these words say about who is welcome to investigate Jesus' birth and celebrate Him.

On the very first Christmas visit, the people who came looking for Jesus weren't Bible teachers or church folk. Nor were they from the same culture or even the same country as the Savior. But that didn't stop the Magi from coming. And no one turned them away when they knocked on the door.

For some people today, Jesus seems like a foreigner. His message of humility and selflessness doesn't square with modern society. His mission to free people from bondage to sin sounds antiquated. And church "culture" sometimes looks like a different world. Even people who believe in Jesus feel alienated at times because of the circumstances in our lives.

But hear this: Jesus was never one to check pedigrees or resumés. He welcomed the wealthy and the poor, the sick and the strong, the respected and the shunned, men and women, adults and children, Jews and gentiles. The same is true today. No matter who you are, the simple call is the same: *come.*

So don't let anything stop you from journeying toward Jesus. Not your culture or your creed. Not your past mistakes or your future fears. Not your level of learning or how you make your living. Just join the Magi on a new adventure – even invite another "foreigner" to come along – all the while keeping the true destination in focus. Not a tree or presents or even a beautiful candlelight church service. But the very Christ Himself, God's Anointed.

Come and see.

Pray to seek Jesus as the Magi did. Just as their journey brought them closer and closer to their encounter with the Son of God, pray that you will be drawn more strongly with each day, not to the bright lights of a commercial holiday, but to a personal encounter with the brilliant Light of the World.

"We saw his star as it rose,
and we have come to worship him."
Matthew 2:2 NLT

"I see him, but not now;
I perceive him, but not near.
A star will come from Jacob,
and a scepter will arise from Israel.
He will smash the forehead of Moab
and strike down all the Shethites.
Edom will become a possession;
Seir will become a possession of its enemies,
but Israel will be triumphant.
One who comes from Jacob will rule...
Numbers 24:17-19a HCSB

"They were the ones who followed Balaam's advice
and were the means of turning the Israelites away from the LORD...
so that a plague struck the LORD's people.
Numbers 31:16 NIV

Day Four
Assurance of Things Hoped For

It's not surprising that the Magi noticed a new star in the sky. They were royal astronomers, after all. But how did these Persian stargazers recognize the connection between a new light in the sky, Daniel's prophecy (*Day Two*), and a newborn in Judea? A connection so profound that they would drop everything to lead a caravan on a two-year trek through the desert?

Well, perhaps you've heard of Balaam. He was a gentile soothsayer hired by Moab to curse Israel as they approached the Promised Land. When Balaam traveled to meet the Moabite king, he experienced the infamous incident with his talking donkey: in a humiliating turn of events, the donkey could see the Angel of the Lord blocking their path, while the "seer" could not.[5]

Humbled and shaken, Balaam proceeded to share four oracles from God with the Moabites concerning Israel. The words Balaam proclaimed were a far cry from the ones the king had paid him to proclaim.

✻ Read the verses on the opposite page (the Numbers 24 passage is from Balaam's fourth oracle; the Numbers 31 passage tells the rest of his story).

Balaam's story is a curious case. He refused Moab's riches in order to proclaim God's blessing on Israel. Yet shortly thereafter, Balaam turned around and advised the Midianites how best to lead God's children astray. In the final analysis, Balaam allowed God to *use* him, but not to *change* him.

Despite Balaam's lack of personal faith and his ultimate downfall, God still chose to use him in a mighty way. Even after Balaam's death, God's people were reminded of his oracles time and again. First in Joshua, as they prepared to take Canaan.[6] Then in Nehemiah, as they returned from exile.[7] And again in Micah,[8] sandwiched between messianic promises and accusations of sin. We read about Balaam still more in 2 Peter, Jude, and Revelation.[9]

It was Balaam's oracle that clicked in the Magi's minds, forming a constellation between prophecies spoken and now fulfilled. In the days ahead, we will dig into the meaning of Balaam's words. Today, though, let us celebrate the fact that we worship a God so great that He can and does use whomever He chooses to accomplish His purposes – whether that person has strong faith or weak faith or no faith at all.

Pray that the Lord would take your faith – whether it is as deep as the ocean or as small as a mustard seed – and grow it for both your good and His glory.

Then the LORD took Abram outside and said to him,
"Look up into the sky and count the stars if you can.
That's how many descendants you will have!"

Genesis 15:5 NLT

"The LORD your God has multiplied you, and behold,
you are this day like the stars of heaven in number."

Deuteronomy 1:10 NASB

"I will make the descendants of David my servant and the Levites who
minister before me as countless as the stars in the sky
and as measureless as the sand on the seashore."

Jeremiah 33:22 NIV

"...There shall come forth [*darak*] a star [*kohkav*] out of Jacob..."
Numbers 24:17 ASV

Day Five
Twinkle, Twinkle...

God certainly loves stars. He placed a multitude of them in the sky to awe us and to guide our way through the night. He also used them to make outrageous promises to His children.

✻ Read the verses on the opposite page.

Time and again, the Creator promised aging, childless Abraham that his descendants would number the stars. Five hundred years later, the Israelites crossed the Jordan into the Promised Land, with a population of about two million[10] people! The promise of *many* stars had most definitely been fulfilled.

But what about the prophecy of the *one* star? What could Balaam's oracle mean? Surely a literal ball of fire wouldn't rise up from the dirt of the Promised Land – or would it? And whatever the "star" was, what would it do?

Balaam said the star would *darak*: "come out" or "rise." *Darak* is a rich, action-packed word. Found throughout the Old Testament in many different contexts,[11] *darak's* definition paints quite a picture: This star from Jacob's descendants would *tread* the earth with its feet. It would *guide* and *lead* with mercy. And it would *thresh* and *string a bow* with righteous vengeance.

Certainly these sound more like the actions of a powerful man than a celestial ball of fire. The truth is, it is *both*. While *kohkav* does literally mean "star," the figurative meaning of the Hebrew word is "prince." Even – according to Jewish and Christian scholars alike[12] – the *Messianic* prince.

In His infinite grace and wisdom, God gave Balaam a prophecy that was both literal and figurative. Perhaps that way, no one would miss it. And so, when the time was full, the Lord put a blazing star in the sky in order to light the Magi's way to the very Light of the World: the Messianic King who would walk the earth to guide, to rise, and, ultimately, to rule.

In Isaiah 48:17, the Lord calls Himself our Redeemer, who will personally lead – *darak* – us in the right direction. Pray that your heart and mind will be open to where God is leading you, knowing that He has tread – *darak* – the same earth that you have, and knowing that He will ultimately thresh – *darak* – the evil in this world. Your job is to follow His Light.

"...a Sceptre shall spring up from Israel..."
Numbers 24:17 DRA

Even when I walk through the darkest valley,
I will not be afraid, for you are close beside me.
Your rod and your staff protect and comfort me.

Psalm 23:4 NLT

A shoot will come up from the stump of Jesse;
from his roots a Branch will bear fruit.
The Spirit of the LORD will rest on him—
the Spirit of wisdom and of understanding,
the Spirit of counsel and of power,
the Spirit of knowledge and of the fear of the LORD -
and he will delight in the fear of the LORD.
He will not judge by what he sees with his eyes,
or decide by what he hears with his ears;
but with righteousness he will judge the needy,
with justice he will give decisions for the poor of the earth.
He will strike the earth with the rod of his mouth;
with the breath of his lips he will slay the wicked.
Righteousness will be his belt
and faithfulness the sash around his waist.

Isaiah 11:1-4a NIV

Day Six
Carry a Big Stick

Why is it that monarchs always wield a scepter? Whether it is God's scepter of righteousness or His rod of wrath, even the ungodly's scepter of wickedness[13] or Hollywood's bejeweled staff, kings always carry a big stick. The rising Star from Jacob was no different.

The Hebrew word for Scepter, rod and staff is *shevet* - literally, a "branch." But in the hands of a leader, it becomes a symbol of authority, whether used as a royal pointer[14] or a weapon of war."[15]

This mighty rod is the exact same *shevet* that comforted David in the twenty-third Psalm. It should be an overwhelming comfort to know that the same King who reigns with the fiercest righteousness also guides with the sweetest tenderness those whose hearts are His. Yet the rod of David's Lord would do more than comfort His children and strike down the wicked.

✳ Read the passages on the opposite page.

Isaiah's powerful prophecy told the world so much about the Lord's Anointed. The prophet foretold the Messiah's lineage, His nature, His rescue, and His peace. Isaiah also tells us that the *shevet* of the Messiah's mouth will strike the earth. It should be no surprise to learn that Jewish scholars say that the use of *shevet* here and in Balaam's oracle don't refer to a physical *stick* of authority. Instead, *shevet* refers to *words* of authority coming from the Messiah Himself.[16]

Isaiah's and Balaam's *shevet* is not a mere *symbol* of authority, power, guidance and righteousness. This *shevet* is literally a living, breathing, majestic Person.

Indeed, just as *shevet* can mean "branch," the Scepter of whom Balaam spoke would be the Shoot from the stump of Jesse. He would be the mortal branching off of the Divine Trinity. The Branch would be the tangible personification of every aspect of the Almighty's scepter: His righteous authority, His tender mercy, and His words of Truth.

Indeed, the scepter would be *The Word Himself* made flesh.

Honor the Almighty today for His authority and His righteousness.
Ask Him to guide you with His wisdom and His purpose. Seek comfort in His
love and His mercy. Kneel at the touch of God's Scepter
and receive all that He has in loving and perfect store for you.

Genesis 49:10

"The sceptre shall not depart from Judah...
until Shiloh come..." (ASV)

The scepter shall never depart from Judah... While tribute
is brought to him, and he receives the people's homage. (NAB)

The scepter will not depart from Judah, nor the ruler's staff
from his descendants, until the coming of the one to whom it belongs, the
one whom all nations will honor. (NLT)

The scepter or leadership shall not depart from Judah...until Shiloh [the
Messiah, the Peaceful One] comes to Whom it belongs, and to Him shall
be the obedience of the people. (AMP)

The scepter shall not be taken away from Juda...till he come that is to be
sent and he shall be the expectation of the nations. (DR)

The scepter turneth not aside from Judah...
till his seed come... (YLT)

The scepter shall not depart from Judah...
as long as men come to Shiloh... (NAB)

Day Seven
Deja Vu

Balaam's prophecy was outlandish. This band of Hebrews, a nation born out of slavery and living as nomads, would produce the ruler of humanity! Who could have imagined this promise for Jacob's seed? Actually, *Jacob* did.

✵ Read Genesis 49:10 in the seven translations on the opposite page.

As Jacob lay on his deathbed, the twelve tribes didn't exist. There were just twelve sons and their families preparing to grieve. The man who once saw angels ascending and descending a ladder to heaven was now poised to finally go there.

As he blessed each son that day, Jacob the father became Israel the patriarch, looking beyond his own small family to the larger plan for the family of God. Jacob proclaimed that the offspring of his third son, Judah, would wield authority over the rest of his descendants. And for how long? Well, until *Shiloh* comes.

No one agrees exactly how to translate Genesis 49:10. *Shiloh* could be a combination of the words *shai* (tribute) and *loh* (to him). Or, if you change the Hebrew vowel markings, the word becomes *shellow*, which means "that which belongs to him." It could even refer to the biblical city that was home to the ancient Tabernacle.[17] Or, according to ancient Jewish texts and teaching, *Shiloh* refers to the Messiah Himself.[18]

In truth, no matter which of these ways you translate Jacob's *Shiloh*, it still pointed to the Christ: the One from Judah to whom all tribute will ultimately be given; the One who will one day wield the scepter belonging to Him alone; the One who became the Tabernacle made flesh – God's living, breathing Presence among us. The Messiah.

Jacob's blessing and Balaam's oracle were bookends to 250 years of captivity and wandering. Their promises sustained Jacob's descendants through trials, and then energized them as they approached the Promised Land. The prophecies also held monumental promise for all of mankind. And when the Magi saw that new star rising in the night sky, they knew the Scepter was being handed down for the last time. *Shiloh* had finally arrived.

> Consider God's precious promises to each person who seeks refuge in His loving authority: to lead us, to remain with us and to protect us eternally. His faithfulness never falters. Trust in that and cling to it, for God's promises are for your good and for eternity.

"Out of Jacob shall come He
who will have dominion..."

Numbers 24:19 KJ21

David also defeated the Moabites.
He put garrisons throughout Edom, and all the Edomites became subject
to David. The Lord gave David victory wherever he went.

2 Samuel 8:2a,14 NIV

THE LORD (God) says to my Lord (the Messiah), Sit at My right hand,
until I make Your adversaries Your footstool.
The Lord will send forth from Zion the scepter of Your strength; Rule,
then, in the midst of Your foes.

Psalm 110:1-2 AMP (of David)

_____

I shall see Him, but not now; I shall behold Him, but it is not near.
When the mighty King of Jakob's house shall reign, and the
Meshiha, the Power-sceptre of Israel, be anointed...
A King is to arise from the house of Jakob, and a Redeemer
and Ruler from the house of Israel...

from Numbers 22-25, Targum Jonathan[19]

Day Eight
The Rising Ruler

T he people receiving Balaam's promise of a rising, redeeming King were a band of freed slaves who had been roaming around in the wilderness for decades. Jacob's descendants hadn't even set foot in the Promised Land yet. And it would be more than 400 years before they would have any king at all, let alone one who would wield global dominion.

Yet the Almighty promised that one of Jacob's descendants would rise to conquer Israel's greatest enemies. This King would have complete dominion – literally to subdue and tread the nations down with his feet like a winepress.

But by the time our Magi came along, hadn't the oracle already been fulfilled?

✹ Read the first three passages on the opposite page.

In Jewish teaching, there is universal agreement that Balaam's prophecy was fulfilled *in part* through David's defeat of Edom and Moab. The greatest king in Israel's history, Judah's descendant subdued the nations around him. Balaam's four-hundred-year-old prophecy had been fulfilled.

Yet, taught the rabbis, like so many prophecies, Balaam's oracle held both a short-term and a long-term promise.[20] In fact, not even victorious King David believed he was the complete fulfillment of the promise. The "man after God's own heart"[21] understood that God's ultimate plan was not about *him*.

And so, hundreds of years later, when Israel was carried off to Babylon, the Jews still clung to Balaam's promise, waiting for another star to rise—*the* Star.

✹ Read Balaam's oracle on the opposite page, as taught during the exile in Babylon – more than six hundred years *after* David's death.

God's people knew that He would deliver completely on His promise, but not with an earthly king. Instead, the promised Star would be the Redeemer Messiah who would come to reign both inside their hearts and over all the nations.

What kind of ruler are you following today? Political, economic, emotional, or eternal? No matter how wise, powerful or loving an earthly leader may be, he or she cannot perfectly guide, protect, or love. Either in word or in deed or in death, human beings will inevitably fail. Choose, then, to seek and follow the Ruler who has the highest wisdom and the deepest love and the mightiest power to shepherd you through all circumstances without fail, for all time.

Balaam then arose and went back to his homeland.

Numbers 24:25 HCSB

...all the leaders of the priests and the people became more and
more unfaithful... The LORD, the God of their fathers, sent word to
them...again and again, because he had pity on his people...But they
mocked God's messengers, despised his words
and scoffed at his prophets until the wrath of the LORD was aroused
against his people and there was no remedy.
He brought up against them the king of the Babylonians,
who killed their young men with the sword in the sanctuary, and spared
neither young man nor young woman, old man or aged.
God handed all of them over to Nebuchadnezzar.

2 Chronicles 36:14-17 NIV

The people of Zion said, "The LORD has turned away and forgotten us."
The LORD answered, "Could a mother...fail to love an infant who came
from her own body? Even if a mother could forget, I will never forget
you... I have set a time when I will help by coming to save you.
I have chosen you to take my promise of hope to other nations. You will
rebuild the country from its ruins, then people will come and settle there...
I will soon give a signal for the nations to return your sons and your
daughters to the arms of Jerusalem...
You won't be disappointed if you trust in me."

Isaiah 49:8,14-16,23b CEV

Day Nine
Exile

O n his way back to Mesopotamia, perhaps Balaam stopped at Israel's encampment to share his prophecies. Or maybe Israel had spies posted within Moab, and they brought back the news. No matter how Balaam's story made its way to Moses and the people, his prophecies became part of God's enduring, Holy Word.

Yet Balaam's oracles did not remain cloistered in the desert, known only to the Israelites. We learn from Numbers that Balaam returned home to Mesopotamia, the region of Babylon, where others would surely hear his proclamation of Judah's future reign. You may recall that something else was carried off to Babylon a few hundred years later: the nation of Israel.

✳ Read the verses on the opposite page.

There is no question that the exile was a painful, devastating period of time for God's people. Sometimes, as it was with the Israelites, exile from God's blessings is the result of our own disobedience. At other times, we feel dragged into exile because we've been hit by the wake of someone else's sin. And sometimes, even when the Lord is right beside us, it feels like we're in exile when we experience the harsh realities of life in a fallen world.

But even in the midst of pain, and even in the midst of punishment, the Almighty uses people who are dedicated to Him to accomplish amazing things. Just think of the powerful testimonies of Esther and of Daniel, and of Shadrach, Meshach and Abednego, during the exile in Babylon.

In fact, it was during the exile that God made His famous promise through Jeremiah: *"For I know the plans I have for you," says the Lord. "Plans to prosper you and not to harm you. Plans to give you a hope and a future."*[22] That future included the exiles' return home, and that hope included the coming Messiah.

The Lord spoke some of the greatest messianic prophecies in all of Scripture through people living in the midst of exile. He can speak just as powerfully and just as tenderly in the midst of yours.

Are you feeling exiled from someone or some place, or even from God?
Think about Daniel, Esther, and the three in the fire. God can use your time of
pain to bring you closer to Him, and perhaps to bring others along with you,
if you will seek and honor Him. Pray that He will help you do so.

"And who knows but that you have come
to the kingdom for such a time as this
and for this very occasion?"

Esther 4:14 AMP

For we are God's masterpiece.
He has created us anew in Christ Jesus,
so we can do the good things
he planned for us long ago.

Ephesians 2:10 NLT

You did not choose me, but I chose you
and appointed you to go and bear fruit —
fruit that will last.

John 15:16a NIV

Work at everything you do with all your heart.
Work as if you were working for the Lord, not for human masters.

Colossians 3:23 NIRV

For Such a Time as This

Balaam's prophecy confirmed Jacob's blessing of Judah. It also identified a tangible sign – the star – to let people know when the Messiah arrived. So who recognized the sign? Apparently no one in Israel, because it took inquiring foreigners to prompt an inquiry among the Messiah's own people.

Perhaps God put the Christmas star in the sky where only people in Persia could see it. Maybe people in Israel saw the star, but chose to ignore it since God warned them not to worship the heavenly bodies.[23] Or maybe, weary and beaten down by countless occupiers and overlords, Israel had given up looking for the sign.

But the Magi simply could not disregard this star. Recall who the Magi were and what they did. These men were *astronomers*. They spent their lives studying the night sky. The Magi were therefore in the perfect place to recognize Balaam's promised sign: the rising star from Jacob, or *Israel*.

The Magi's daily grind became the means through which the Lord gave them their greatest gift.

✳ Read the passages on the opposite page.

The Lord placed Esther, an unknown Jewish girl, on the throne of Persia for a specific, divine purpose that she never could have forseen: to save her people, God's people. Five hundred years later, God put a group of wealthy astronomers in Persia for a specific, divine purpose: to greet His Son, the Messiah, who had come to save His people, all people.

God speaks to each of His children in ways we uniquely understand. For the Magi, it was the stars. Their hearts must have raced as they connected the brilliant new star with Balaam's messianic oracle. And they must have known at the depths of their souls that they had been prepared for such a time as this.

What is your occupation? How has God gifted you? Are you a teacher, a doctor, a plumber? Are you skilled in athletics or writing or art? Whatever your job or gift is, it has been given to you from the Lord with something very special in mind. Delight in it, and ask God to meet you there so you can feel His Presence and use your gift to bless others. You never know when He will turn something mundane into something monumental.

By day the LORD went ahead of them in a pillar of cloud
to guide them...and by night in a pillar of fire
to give them light, so that they could travel by day or night.

Exodus 13:21 NIV

[The blind man] said, Lord, let me receive my sight!
And Jesus said to him, Receive your sight!
...And instantly he received his sight and began to follow Jesus,
recognizing, praising, and honoring God;
and all the people, when they saw it, praised God.

Luke 18:41-43 AMP

"There is a boy here who has five small loaves...and two fish. But what
good is that with all these people?" Jesus...gave thanks to God. Then he
passed the bread to the people and he did the same with the fish, until
everyone had plenty to eat. After the people had seen Jesus work this
miracle, they began saying,
"This must be the Prophet who is to come into the world!"

John 6:9,11,14 CEV

"This sickness will not end in death but is for the glory of God,
so that the Son of God may be glorified through it." He shouted with a
loud voice, "Lazarus, come out!" The dead man came out bound hand and
foot with linen strips...Therefore many of the Jews who came to Mary and
saw what He did believed in Him.

John 11:4,43-45 HCSB

Day Eleven
Miracles

There are a multitude of theories about the Christmas star. Among the most popular: planets aligning, comets traveling through and supernovas exploding. But *this* star did things that ordinary stars and comets cannot. It stopped and started. It moved in different directions. It hovered over a *single house* in Bethlehem.[24] This was no ordinary star.

The star pursued by the Magi was – in both its purpose and its Source – the same as the pillar of fire and the cloud that led the Israelites through the wilderness. On the way to the Promised Land, God descended in the form of the fire and the cloud to lead His people along the path He had set out for them. Fifteen hundred years later, God's illuminating Presence lit the Magi's way on their journey to His Son, the promised Light of the World.

✻ Read the passages on the opposite page.

The Magi's journey began with something very familiar to them: a star. But this star was completely outside the realm of the everyday cosmic routine. In other words, it was a miracle. And God's miracles always have a purpose. In truth, His miracles always serve a *dual* purpose. First, they meet a tangible – usually overwhelming – personal need. And in meeting that deep need, the miracle in turn brings glory to the Miracle Maker.

Consider the fire and the cloud. The loaves and the fishes. The healing of a blind man and the raising of Lazarus. In each circumstance, God met a personal need in a way that turned countless hearts toward Him. The miracles cried out, "Look at Me! I can meet any need – beyond what you can even begin to imagine! So seek me with all you've got: your mind, your heart, your strength and your soul."

And that's exactly what the Magi did in response to this miracle. Their stargazing minds stirred up their hearts and their strength in order to seek the One who would capture their souls.

Have you ever experienced a miracle? Are you in need of one now? Ask the Creator to send one into your life to meet your need, whether large or small. Ask Him to take something ordinary in your life and turn it into something extraordinary in such a way that will reveal His love and His power more deeply, more strongly, and more personally than ever before.

"...thou shalt love Jehovah thy God with all thy heart,
and with all thy soul, and with all thy strength."

Deuteronomy 6:5 Darby

"Bring all the tithes into the storehouse so there will be enough food in
my Temple. If you do," says the Lord of Heaven's Armies,
"I will open the windows of heaven for you. I will pour out a blessing so
great you won't have enough room to take it in!
Try it! Put me to the test!"

Malachi 3:10 NLT

"The place where your treasure is,
is the place you will most want to be, and end up being."

Matthew 6:21 The Message

Each of you must bring a gift in proportion to the way
the LORD your God has blessed you.

Deuteronomy 16:17 NIV

Since we have gifts that differ according to the grace given to us,
each of us is to exercise them accordingly: if prophecy, according to the
proportion of his faith; if service, in his serving; or he who teaches,
in his teaching; or he who exhorts, in his exhortation; he who gives,
with liberality; he who leads, with diligence; he who shows mercy,
with cheerfulness.

Romans 12:6-8 NASB

Day Twelve
Where is Your Treasure?

A rmed with their stargazing skill and great expectations, the Magi set off after the star. While we don't know how many Magi there were (eastern tradition says twelve,[25] while western claims three) we *do* know how many gifts they brought.

There is rich symbolism in each of the three treasures, which we will explore in the days ahead. It is unlikely that the Magi chose their gifts with any messianic symbolism in mind. It *is* certain, however, that God can and does use His creation to accomplish things of which they aren't even aware.

For example, Joseph wasn't trying to fulfill prophecy[26] when he packed up his pregnant wife and rode to Bethlehem; he was simply following orders from Rome. The Roman soldiers didn't know they were fulfilling Jewish prophecy[27] when they cast lots for Jesus' clothes, they just wanted some loot. And the Temple leadership certainly didn't pay Judas thirty pieces of silver for his betrayal of Jesus because they desired to fulfill messianic foreshadowing.[28] They just wanted the job done.

Likewise, the Magi didn't know there was a deeper purpose in their gifts of gold and frankincense and myrrh. They were simply bringing the newborn King the finest substances their nation had to offer.[29]

✴ Read the passages on the opposite page.

No, the Magi did not choose gold, frankincense and myrrh out of intentional symbolism. They were simply compelled to bring the long-awaited King the most valuable gifts they could possibly offer. And that is exactly what the Lord asks of us: not necessarily to understand, but in obedience to give Him our very best.

The Magi's willingness to bring Jesus their very best opened the way for them to receive an even greater treasure, the most valuable treasure of all: a personal relationship with the Lord of Heaven.

Bring God the very best that you have. Spend time in prayer and His Word not with your very last ounce of energy, but with focus and anticipation. Joyfully bring Him your tithe off the top, not the crumbs from the bottom. Do you have a wealth of words? Write an encouraging note. An abundance of time? Offer it to a needy neighbor. Whatever God has given you, He has blessed you in order to be a blessing to others. So give the best of it away.

"Where can we find and pay homage to the newborn
King of the Jews? We observed a star in the
eastern sky that signaled his birth.
We're on a pilgrimage to worship him."
They entered the house and saw the child
in the arms of Mary, his mother.
Overcome, they kneeled and worshipped him.
Then they opened their luggage and presented gifts:
gold, frankincense, myrrh.

Matthew 2:2,11 The Message

"I saw a human form, a son of man, arriving in a whirl of clouds.
He came to The Old One and was presented to him. He was given
power to rule—all the glory of royalty. Everyone—race,
color, and creed—had to serve him. His rule would be forever,
never ending. His kingly rule would never be replaced."

Daniel 7:14 The Message

Jesus said, "My kingdom is not of this world...
for this reason I was born, and for this
I came into the world, to testify to the truth."

John 18:36-37 NIV

And on His robe and on His thigh He has a name written,
"KING OF KINGS, AND LORD OF LORDS."

Revelation 19:16 NASB

Day Thirteen
Kingmakers

G old. It is a beautiful treasure commonly bestowed on royalty as an expression of honor and submission. It makes perfect sense, then, that gold coated most of the Lord's Tabernacle and His Temple. He is, after all, the King of Kings. And so it was only fitting that the Magi presented it to the newborn King in Bethlehem.

✳ Read the verses on the opposite page.

Because of Balaam's oracle and Daniel's prophecy, the Magi knew that Jesus would not only be King of the Jews, but that He would also be *their* King – the King of *all* the nations. Their gift of gold expressed their honor and their submission to His ultimate authority.

It made no difference that the Messiah sat in a highchair rather than on a throne. The Magi came in recognition of Jesus' ultimate kingship, just as Samuel anointed David as king twenty years before he would assume the throne.

Jesus didn't have to earn His authority or grow into it. He was born to rule.

Acknowledging Jesus' kingship was actually part of the Magi's job description. In addition to serving as royal astronomers and scientists, the Magi were kingmakers. Literally. No one received the throne in Persia without first being approved, and then crowned, by magi.[30]

So when they sought out the newborn Messiah, our Magi came armed with their authority as kingmakers. And in doing so, these Persians placed an official, Gentile seal of approval on Jesus. They presented Jesus their gift of gold, acknowledging that He was, indeed, *the* King. King of the nation that hadn't noticed His birth. King of the earth that was created by His unseen Hand. And King of the entire world that would one day be rescued by His outstretched Arms.

"Who is he, this King of glory?" asked David rhetorically. "The Lord Almighty—he is the King of glory."[31] Is He yours?

> Have you crowned Jesus as King in your heart and your mind?
> Does He reign in your thoughts and words and actions?
> Pray about areas of your life where you could submit more fully to His lordship,
> that He might lead you and bless you in ways you haven't begun to imagine.

Then they opened up their treasure chests and
gave him gifts of gold, frankincense, and myrrh.

Matthew 2:11b NLT

"Take for yourself spices...with pure frankincense...
With it you shall make incense, a perfume...
...it shall be most holy to you."

Exodus 30:34–36 NASB

Jesus was going throughout all Galilee, teaching in their synagogues
and proclaiming the gospel of the kingdom,
and healing every kind of disease
and every kind of sickness among the people.

Matthew 4:23 NASB

So then, since we have a great High Priest who has entered heaven, Jesus
the Son of God, let us hold firmly to what we believe.
This High Priest of ours understands our weaknesses,
for he faced all of the same testings we do, yet he did not sin.
So let us come boldly before the throne of our gracious God.
There we will receive his mercy, and we will find grace
to help us when we need it most.

Hebrews 4:14–16 NLT

Day Fourteen
The Highest of All Priests

Frankincense held a prominent place throughout the ministry of God's House – first in the Tabernacle, and then in the Jerusalem Temple. Priests sprinkled it on grain offerings and on the holy Shewbread kept in the sanctuary. Frankincense was also the most prominent ingredient in the Lord's holy incense, which burned both night and day in the sanctuary.

✲ Read the passages on the opposite page.

According to God's design, the Old Testament priests served to bridge the gap between man and God. The Magi's gift of frankincense, so important in the priests' ministry, pointed clearly to Jesus' role as our Great High Priest. Indeed, throughout His life, Jesus encouraged men, women, and children to turn their hearts to the Lord, closing the gap between them. And then, on the Cross, Jesus performed the ultimate priestly duty, offering a perfect sacrifice – Himself – to pay the Old Testament price for sin.[32]

The Magi's frankincense beautifully foreshadowed the fact that Jesus would become our Great High Priest. But the gift did even more than that. It actually pointed to what the life of our Great High Priest would look like.

The value of frankincense went far beyond its beautiful fragrance. It is medicinal. Frankincense is actually a stimulant,[33] used throughout history to treat everything from tumors to laryngitis to leprosy.[34]

Our Jesus was literally the living Frankincense: His life continually rose in a pleasing aroma to His Father as He worked spiritual and physical healing on earth. His touch and His words restored the leper, gave voice to the mute, and even brought the dead back to life.

When the Magi bestowed their gift of fragrant, medicinal frankincense, they surely could not have imagined that Jesus would one day cure death itself. Yet He did. And now, our Great High Priest continues to minister on our behalf from on high, as the aroma of His victory fills the heavens.

Do you need someone to minister to your soul today? Are you in need of forgiveness, of healing, of restoration, of blessing? If so, approach the Great High Priest who sits at the Almighty's right Hand. He has already offered the sacrifice on your behalf, and now He longs to comfort you, to heal you, to forgive you, and to bless you. All you need to do is ask in faith.

"Take for yourself the finest spices...liquid myrrh...
fragrant cinnamon...fragrant cane...cassia...and...olive oil.
Prepare from these a holy anointing oil...
Anoint Aaron and his sons and
consecrate them to serve Me as priests."

Exodus 30:23-25, 30 NIV

Now the LORD said to Samuel, "...fill your horn with oil and go;
Then Samuel took the horn of oil and anointed [David]
in the midst of his brothers; and the Spirit of the LORD
came mightily upon David from that day forward...

1 Samuel 16:1,13 NASB

[Joseph of Arimathea] was accompanied by Nicodemus...
Nicodemus brought a mixture of myrrh and aloes...
Taking Jesus' body, the two of them wrapped it,
with the spices, in strips of linen...

John 19:39-40 NIV

Live a life filled with love, following the example of Christ. He loved us
and offered himself as a sacrifice for us, a pleasing aroma to God.

Ephesians 5:2 NLT

O death, where is thy sting?
O grave, where is thy victory?
1 Corinthians 15:55 KJV

Day Fifteen
Anointed Unto Death

Pure liquid myrrh was incredibly valuable. In small amounts, it often accompanied other spices in incense mixtures. But this "flowing myrrh" stood out as the main ingredient in God's recipe for holy anointing oil.

❋ Read the passages on the opposite page.

When the Magi arrived at Joseph's and Mary's doorstep, they bestowed this precious gift of anointing to the young Messiah. Perhaps they reverently presented it to Him, sealed in a beautifully ornate alabaster flask. Or, maybe the Magi broke open a small jar and poured flowing myrrh over the toddler's head, letting it drench his curls and drip from His chin. What a magnificent sight that would have been!

To what did the Magi anoint young Jesus? Given along with the gold, the myrrh anointed Jesus as the King. Coupled with the frankincense, the myrrh anointed Jesus as the Priest. But this gift of myrrh didn't just accentuate the Magi's other gifts. As an embalming agent,[35] the myrrh also anointed Jesus as the Sacrifice. The King of Kings and Priest of Priests was born to die.

Jesus' earthly mission was a bitter pill to swallow. And, in fact, myrrh does taste bitter. The Hebrew name for it even comes from the word for bitter: *maror*. No one can deny that as Jesus walked the earth, He tasted the bitterness of life in a fallen world: the arrogance and attacks of religious leaders; the beheading of His cousin, John the Baptist; Judas' betrayal; and Peter's denial. Ultimately, Jesus tasted the bitterness of death on a Cross.

And yet, while myrrh tastes bitter, it smells magnificent. We find it throughout the Songs of Solomon and the Psalms as a perfume and deodorant. It was even part of Queen Esther's beauty treatments.[36] Myrrh's sweet aroma is what made it an ideal substance for embalming – it covered the smell of decay.

These conflicting qualities of myrrh speak so strongly of the Messiah. Despite the bitterness of His earthly mission, Jesus' perfect, obedient life continually rose in a beautiful aroma to His Father. And ultimately, Jesus did not just cover the stench of death, but He took it away completely. The bitterness of death is no more for those filled with and covered by the aroma of Christ.

In the sweetness of manger scenes, it can be easy to forget that Jesus entered the world to pay the price for our sin: death. This season, as you sing of the babe, choose also to remember the Cross, the bitter, yet beautiful Cross.

"Take for yourself spices...stacte [the finest myrrh[37]]...
with pure frankincense... With it you shall make incense, a
perfume...pure, and holy. ...You shall make an altar as a place for
burning incense......you shall overlay it with pure gold...
You shall put this altar in front of the veil that is near the ark of the
testimony, in front of the mercy seat that is over the ark of the testimony,
where I will meet with you... Aaron shall burn fragrant incense on it; he
shall burn it every morning...[and]...at twilight... There shall be
perpetual incense before the LORD throughout your generations...
Aaron shall make atonement on it with the blood of the sin offering once
a year...It is most holy to the LORD."

Exodus 30:34,1,3,6-8,10 NASB

And the LORD said to Moses, "Tell Aaron...not to come at just any time
into the Holy Place behind the veil, before the mercy seat which is on the
ark, lest he die; for I will appear in the cloud above the mercy
seat...Then...with his hands full of sweet incense beaten fine, [Aaron shall]
bring it inside the veil. And he shall put the incense on the fire
before the LORD, that the cloud of incense may cover the
mercy seat that is on the Testimony, lest he die.
...Then he shall...bring [the] blood [of the sin offering] inside the
veil...and sprinkle it on the mercy seat and before the mercy seat.
So he shall make atonement for the Holy Place because of the
uncleanness of the children of Israel...for all their sins ...

Leviticus 16:2,12-13,15-16 NKJV

The Aroma of Atonement

O n their own, each of the Magi's gifts foretold a powerful image of the Messiah: the King, the Priest, and the Sacrifice. But these three gifts were joined together long before the Magi brought them to Jesus. There is a sacred place in Scripture where gold, frankincense and myrrh mingled together. It is a place that endured from the desert wilderness to the days of our Christ, and it painted a breathtaking picture of the coming Savior.

❋ Read the first passage on the opposite page, which is a portion of God's instructions for constructing the desert Tabernacle.

The altar of incense: the *golden* table from which *frankincense* and *myrrh* rose in a pleasing aroma to the Lord. Day and night, night and day, 1,500 years before He set foot on the soil He created, Christ's aroma rose to the heavens. The fragrance of the Messiah continually permeated the Holy of Holies, where the Almighty Himself dwelled.[38] Father and Son were joined as one, even then.

❋ Read the second passage on the opposite page.

The Mercy Seat: the place where God promised His Shekinah glory would dwell, keeping Him close to His children. But the Father's earthly dwelling place was off-limits to everyone except the high priest. And even he was only allowed to enter once each year. On that somber yet beautiful Day of Atonement, the high priest took the holy incense – with its frankincense and myrrh – from the golden altar and entered the very Presence of God, offering atonement for the nation with the blood of a perfect lamb.

For centuries before they were born, the Magi's gifts had been coming together year after year, over and over again. The smell of atoning blood mingled with the aroma of frankincense and myrrh on that golden Mercy Seat.

And then came the One who was gold and frankincense and myrrh all together. The perfect Lamb whose blood would make atonement for all mankind, forever. Now the King and the Priest and the Sacrifice are eternally joined, reigning and ministering and atoning for each and every person who chooses to claim Him.

Ponder the mystery of Christ. Pray that the aroma of His majesty and mercy and perfect plan would penetrate your heart and your mind. Allow Him to be your Lord, your pastor, and your ransom, for He is all three. And pray that your life, like His, would rise in an aroma of love, encouragement and truth to bless everyone in your path.

...wise men from the east arrived
unexpectedly in Jerusalem, saying,
"Where is He who has been born King of the Jews?"

Matthew 2:1b-2a HCSB

"Look, I am with you and will watch over you wherever you go.
...I will not leave you until I have done what I have promised you."

Genesis 28:15 HCSB

For this God is our God for ever and ever;
he will be our guide even to the end.

Psalm 48:14 NIV

"You intended to harm me, but God intended it all for good.
He brought me to this position
so I could save the lives of many people."

Genesis 50:20 NLT

Mary remained standing outside the tomb sobbing.
"...they have taken away my Lord,
and I do not know where they have laid Him."

John 20:11a,13b AMP

"Those who seek me early and diligently will find me."

Proverbs 8:17b AMP

Day Seventeen
Adrift

The star must have flickered. For nearly two years, the faithful Magi followed the Messiah's Light. But then, just as they were making their final approach, the star appears to have vanished. Instead of heading straight to Bethlehem, the Magi had to stop and ask for directions. What went through their minds? Confusion? Frustration? Anger? Had the whole journey been for naught?

Sometimes we are so sure God led us to a certain path: a new job, a new ministry, a new direction. And then, *wham*! Onlookers criticize our methods. Loved ones doubt our vision. We may even stumble into sin. We feel adrift.

Life is filled with confusion. Sometimes it's the result of our own bumbling. Sometimes it's because we *are* going in the right direction, prompting Satan to attack. And sometimes, the Lord allows us to drift for awhile in order to grow our faith – or to accomplish something even greater than we had in mind.

✳ Read the verses on the opposite page.

The most well-known journeys had times of disillusionment. God promised Abraham that his descendants would outnumber the stars, yet the man found himself trudging up Mt. Moriah with instructions to sacrifice his only son. Joseph had prophetic dreams of the leadership God had in store for him, yet he ended up sold into slavery and then unjustly imprisoned. And the man people believed to be the Messiah was instead crucified and buried in a tomb.

At any point along these paths, people could have thrown up their hands. "Lord, where are you?" "I'm so sure I heard you, but look at how things have turned out!" "Did I misunderstand you?" "Have you abandoned me?"

But think of how each of these stories ended. God Himself provided a substitute for Isaac on that altar. Joseph went on to save his family and an entire nation from famine. And Jesus' atoning death culminated in His resurrection, rescuing all of mankind from eternal death.

What, then, should we do in life's inevitable seasons of confusion? Exactly what the Magi did: ask for help.

Are you going through a time of confusion or questioning? Then ask for help. Ask God to reveal His promises and encourage you through His Word. Ask for help from a trustworthy friend in Christ, and accept their care for you, whether it's advice, a shoulder, a prayer, or a meal. And keep pushing forward.

So [King Herod] called together all the chief priests and learned men (scribes) of the people and anxiously asked them where the Christ was to be born. They replied to him, In Bethlehem of Judea, for so it is written by the prophet...: And you, Bethlehem, in the land of Judah you are not in any way least or insignificant among the chief cities of Judah; for from you shall come a Ruler (Leader) Who will govern and shepherd My people Israel.

Matthew 2:4-6 AMP

"May you prosper in Ephrathah and be famous in Bethlehem. And may the LORD give you descendants through this young woman..."
Ruth 4:11-12 NLT

"But you, Bethlehem Ephrathah,
Though you are little among the thousands of Judah,
Yet out of you shall come forth to Me the One to be Ruler in Israel,
Whose goings forth are from old, from everlasting.

Micah 5:2 NKJV

———————————————

Jesus replied, I am the Bread of Life. He who comes to Me will never be hungry, and he who believes in and cleaves to and trusts in and relies on Me will never thirst any more...I [Myself] am this Living Bread that came down from heaven.

John 6:35, 51a AMP

"One from Jacob shall have dominion."

Numbers 24:19 NASB

Day Eighteen
The House of Bread

W hen the Magi asked for directions, they received a unanimous response from both the priests and the scribes. Bethlehem, the city of David, was to be the Messiah's birthplace. Their evidence? The words of Micah the prophet, spoken four hundred years earlier.

✷ Read the first three passages on the opposite page.

God had big plans for little Bethlehem. The first clue was in the life of Ruth. Elders proclaimed respect in Ephrathah and fame in Bethlehem for Ruth and Boaz's family as a result of the loyal convert's faith.[39] The first fruit of this blessing was their great grandson: David, the son of Jesse the *Ephrathite* from *Bethlehem.*[40] Then, five hundred years later, Micah foretold an even greater blessing for Ruth's line and for Bethlehem: the *everlasting* King.

Rest assured that Matthew did not twist Micah's prophecy to support his case for Jesus' identity. Jewish leaders taught then and rabbis still teach now that Micah 5 describes the Messianic age.[41] There is absolute agreement that Bethlehem would be the birthplace of the "Messiah Son of David, [Who] will arise with the strength of the Almighty."[42]

✷ Read the last two passages on the opposite page.

Micah proclaimed that the Everlasting Savior would enter our world through Bethlehem. In Hebrew, the town is *Beit-Lechem*, literally the "House of Bread." When the Messiah arrived 400 years later, how did He identify Himself? As the *Bread of Life*. The One who would fill not only our stomachs but our souls. Prophetically, the Hebrew word translated as "dominion" Balaam's oracle (Numbers 24:19) is the very same word used in the Talmud for taking bread out of the oven.[43]

And so, as the first-century Magi set off down the road towards Bethlehem, their hearts turned to the One who had come to have dominion. The One born in the House of Bread. The time was full. The Bread of Life was ready to come out and feed our souls.

Is there an emptiness or an ache in your soul? How are you trying to fill it?
With something material, chemical, relational? In the long run, no earthly thing
can fill the void or satisfy the longings of your heart. Only Jesus can fill it,
because He is the One who created your heart in the first place.
Choose to feast on His love as you celebrate His birth.

A Star Will Rise   T. L Priest   39

Magi from the east arrived in Jerusalem, saying,
"Where is He who has been born King of the Jews?
For we saw His star in the east and have come to worship Him."
Gathering together all the chief priests and scribes of the people,
[Herod] inquired of them where the Messiah was to be born.

Matthew 2:1-2, 4 NASB

There it was—the true Light [was then] coming into the world
[the genuine, perfect, steadfast Light] that illumines every person.
He came into the world,
and though the world was made through Him,
the world did not recognize Him [did not know Him].
He came to that which belonged to Him
[to His own—His domain, creation, things, world],
and they who were His own
did not receive Him and did not welcome Him.

John 1:9-11 AMP

Day Nineteen
Where is He?

W here is He?" the Magi asked. Surely all of Judea was abuzz. The long awaited Messiah had arrived to restore David's throne! Perhaps the boy had already been brought to Jerusalem, where He could grow up in the shadow of the Temple as He prepared to reign.

But that was not the case. It is astounding that the Messiah, the very Son of the Most High God, was living in the midst of His own people and no one noticed. God's brilliant star led a caravan of Gentiles across a continent, but the Light wasn't even noticed by the ones who should have been waiting the most expectantly. Outside of Jesus' family and old Simeon and Anna at the Temple,[44] it doesn't seem that the Messiah's presence made so much as a ripple among God's people.

✳ Read the verses on the opposite page.

It seems astounding to us that no one in Israel seemed to notice the arrival of their long-awaited Messiah. Yet, we are really not so different from them today. Walking through this season of lights, it has become increasingly easy to become oblivious to the Light. People joyfully sing carols they don't really believe. Others dutifully attend churches they don't usually support. And sadly, just like in first century Judea, many recite words without knowing the Word.

With all this talk of Jesus on the *outside*, it is still quite possible not to invite Him *inside*. Even people who do believe in the Christ can get so filled up with the festivities that we become emptied of our faith.

And so, as we draw closer to Christmas, let us not become so satisfied with crèches and carols that we completely miss His Presence. Instead, let us be like the Magi and seek His Light, His face, and His intimate companionship with everything we've got.

Today, there are signs of Jesus everywhere: Christmas cards and yard displays, Christmas carols and school programs. As you walk through this season of lights, be careful not to overlook *the Light*. Open your eyes to God's Presence all around you. Consider anew the meaning of a carol known since childhood. Retell the Christmas story with the wonder of someone hearing it for the very first time. And be prepared to answer those who are searching, if they come and ask you – like the Magi did – "Where is He?"

"Give to the LORD the glory he deserves!
Bring your offering and come into his presence.
Worship the LORD in all his holy splendor.

1 Chronicles 16:29 NLT

Come, let us bow down and worship him.
Let us fall on our knees in front of the Lord our Maker.

Psalm 95:6 NIRV

David got up from the ground... washed, put on lotions...changed his
clothes [and] went to the house of the LORD and worshipped.

2 Samuel 12:20 NIV

Then those who were in the boat worshiped him,
saying "Truly you are the Son of God."
Matthew 14:33 NIV

And so the Lord says, "These people say they are mine. They honor me
with their lips, but their hearts are far from me. And their worship of me
is nothing but man-made rules learned by rote."
Isaiah 29:13 NLT

Therefore, I urge you, brothers, in view of God's mercy, to offer your
bodies as living sacrifices, holy and pleasing to God—
this is your spiritual act of worship.
Romans 12:1 NIV

Day Twenty
True Worship

What a scene it must have been when the Magi and their entourage arrived in Bethlehem! The caravan of wealthy Persians assembled at the carpenter's home, bowed down before his toddler, and unloaded a pile of riches at the boy's feet. What must the neighbors have thought?

For that matter, what were the Magi thinking? Why didn't they wait to bestow gifts until the King was older and in a position to reward them for their allegiance? The answer is pure and simple. The Magi knew this wasn't about them at all. It did not matter one iota whether this little One – fully God and fully boy – was in a position to do anything for them. The Magi worshipped Jesus simply because of who He was, and they absolutely couldn't wait to do it.

✵ Read the verses on the opposite page.

True worship is simply acknowledging who God is and celebrating Him for it. Our lives don't even have to be in good shape to do it. After all, David got up and worshipped the Lord right after accepting his gut-wrenching punishment for adultery and murder. The disciples declared unbridled praise of Jesus after He had just rebuked them for their lack of faith in the storm-tossed boat.

In fact, no matter how beautifully we sing or sacrificially we give, appearing or sounding worshipful is meaningless to God if it doesn't come from an overflow of personal adoration for Him. Pure worship is to acknowledge that God is the greatest gift there is, and then place our hearts and our lives into His hands. Consider The Message translation of Romans 12:1:

> *Take your everyday, ordinary life—your sleeping, eating, going-to-work, and walking-around life—and place it before God as an offering.*

The Magi had no idea when Jesus would rule or if they would be around to see it. What they *did* know was that this child was the long-awaited Messiah, and they were compelled to celebrate it. How much more, then, should we, who have seen the fulfillment of the Promise – the precious blood and resurrection of God's Son – bring Him the most humble and glorious worship?

> Are you concerned with looking worthy *to* worship, rather than simply worshipping the One who is worthy *of* worship? Take time to praise God for Who He is: Creator, Sustainer, Redeemer, Healer, Counselor, Protector…

When [the Magi] had gone, an angel of the Lord appeared to Joseph
in a dream. "Get up," he said, "take the child and his mother
and escape to Egypt. Stay there until I tell you,
for Herod is going to search for the child to kill him."

Matthew 2:13 NIV

When Elijah saw how things were, he ran for dear life...on into the
desert...He came to a lone broom bush and collapsed in its shade, wanting
in the worst way to be done with it all – to just die: "Enough of this, God!
Take my life..." Suddenly an angel shook him awake and said,
"Get up and eat!" He looked around and, to his surprise, right by his
head were a loaf of bread baked on some coals and a jug of water.
He ate the meal and went back to sleep.

1 Kings 19:3–6 The Message

"...your Father knows exactly what you need even before you ask him!"

Matthew 6:8 NLT

"I will always guide you. I will satisfy your needs in a land that is baked by
the sun. I will make you stronger. You will be like a garden that has plenty
of water...like a spring whose water never runs dry."

Isaiah 58:11 NIRV

My God will meet all your needs. He will meet them in keeping with his
wonderful riches that come to you because you belong to Christ Jesus.

Philippians 4:19 NIRV

The Provider

M atthew doesn't describe how Joseph and Mary reacted to the Magi's gifts. The humble couple must have been utterly flabbergasted. After the shock wore off, though, the visit must have been a time of magnificent fellowship. One can imagine them all exchanging powerful prophecies and sweet stories about the little One who was rising from Jacob.

Abruptly, though, at some point during the Magi's stay, the Lord warned the Magi to head home to Persia without reporting back to Herod. And right after the Magi left, Joseph received a similar warning about the deceitful king. So before the sun rose on a new day, Joseph packed up his family and fled to Egypt.

✻ Read Matthew 2:13 on the opposite page

This poor Jewish family was supposed to just drop everything and move to Egypt? Immediately? For an unspecified amount of time? How in the world did the Lord expect Joseph to provide for the needs of his family – especially his child, *the Son of God?* Well, that's easy. With *gold* and *frankincense* and *myrrh*! In God's perfect timing, the Magi's lavish gifts provided the means for Joseph's family to pay for food and shelter[45] during their brief exile.

Our God is not only loving, He is also incredibly practical. He didn't just provide spiritual support to Joseph, Mary, and Jesus. He met their tangible, physical needs. And He did it before they even knew they were in need! So when the Lord said to leave on a sudden journey, right after dropping an unexpected fortune on their doorstep, they knew He was in complete control.

✻ Read the rest of the passages on the opposite page.

When Elijah fled into the desert, the prophet was so depressed and exhausted that he literally wanted to die. But Elijah awoke from his despair to find that God had arranged a little meal for him. When the Creator of the universe knows you're alone in the wilderness and cares enough to fill your rumbling belly, you know that He knows *everything* you're dealing with. And you know that He cares for you. After all, Elijah was His child. And so are you.

Are you in need financially, emotionally, physically? Ask the Lord to meet your needs, and expect the unexpected. He can and will meet your needs in ways you least expect. And His provision – like the Magi's gifts – will bring His Son honor in the process, so that your heart and the hearts of others will be drawn to Him.

"The Son of Man came eating and drinking, and they say, 'Look, a glutton and a drunkard, a friend of tax collectors and sinners!'"
Matthew 11:19 ESV

Simon Peter replied, You are the Christ, the Son of the Living God.
Matthew 16:16 AMP

Then the high priest tore his robes and said, "He has blasphemed!"
Matthew 26:65 NASB

"Rabbi, you are the Son of God; you are the King of Israel."
John 1:49 NIV

When his family heard what was happening, they tried to take him away. "He's out of his mind," they said.
Mark 3:21 NLT

"Yes, Lord," she told him, "I believe that you are the Christ, the Son of God, who was to come into the world."
John 11:27 NIV

"You are demon-possessed," the crowd answered.
John 7:20a NIV

...the centurion...said "Truly this man was the Son of God!"
Mark 15:39 RSV

Day Twenty Two
No Fence Sitting

Rage and indifference. Herod ordered the murder of all the boys Jesus' age, while the religious leaders didn't even accompany the Magi to Bethlehem. Their reactions lead one to wonder if anyone really wanted the Messiah to arrive. Maybe they just relished the *idea* of His arrival, but when the rubber hit the road, they were quite satisfied with the status quo.

❋ Read the different reactions to Jesus recorded on the opposite page.

As Jesus emerged from anonymity, people's reactions to Him didn't change much from those early days. In fact, those same reactions just became more pronounced. Some called Jesus a drunkard. The high priest accused Him of blasphemy. His family thought He'd lost His mind. Worshippers at the Temple declared He was demon-possessed. Others, however – just like the Magi – publicly hailed Jesus as the Son of God, and their lives were never the same.

What about each of us? Do we really want to accept that Jesus stepped into our midst? If we do, then things are going to change. They have to, because Jesus simply cannot enter a life without changing it. Not that He forces us to. We just know deep down that if we accept God's Son, if we love Him and seek Him, we will end up actually *wanting* to change things about our lives. Maybe to even give things up. And that's scary.

So some people ignore Jesus, like the religious leaders did. Others react with hostility, like Herod did. But whether the Jerusalem leadership liked it or not, the King had arrived and was living just down the road. Their reactions had no bearing on the Truth. Neither do ours.

Jesus *is* in our midst. Right now, wherever you are. Just as He was in Bethlehem. Just as He was on the Cross. And just as He was outside the empty tomb. Jesus is *here*. We can choose to be hostile. We can choose to be indifferent. Or, we can claim Him as the Savior He is and embrace Him.

> How do you feel about Jesus? Not about religion, but about Jesus Himself. Are you enamored? Indifferent? Hostile? Do you like the idea of Jesus but not the reality of Him in the Flesh? As we approach the celebration of His birth, examine your heart. How do you feel about the One who came to love and redeem you? If you'd like to know the Savior better, you may want to start by reading the book of John.

The LORD had said to Abram... "I will make you into a great nation
and...all peoples on earth will be blessed through you."

Genesis 12:1-3 NIV

"It is too small a thing for you to be my servant to
restore the tribes of Jacob and bring back those of Israel I have kept. I
will also make you a light for the Gentiles, that you
may bring my salvation to the ends of the earth."

Isaiah 49:6 NIV

He will proclaim peace to the nations. His rule will extend from sea to sea
and from the River to the ends of the earth.

Zechariah 9:10 NIV

...being the high priest that year, Caiaphas prophesied that Jesus was to
die for the nation, and...also for the purpose of uniting into one body the
children of God who have been scattered far and wide.

John 11:51-52 AMP

For there is no difference between Jew and Gentile—
the same Lord is Lord of all and richly blesses all who call on him...

Romans 10:12 NIV

This mystery is that through the gospel the Gentiles are heirs together
with Israel, members together of one body,
and sharers together in the promise in Christ Jesus.

Ephesians 3:6 NIV

Day Twenty Three
Grafted In

The reactions in Jerusalem to Jesus' birth were a foreshadowing of what was to come – not just on a personal level, but on a global scale. Rejected and ignored by most of His own, the Messiah was accepted and worshipped by Gentiles, allowing them to be grafted into His Father's family tree.

✳ Read God's promises of universal salvation on the opposite page.

From the very beginning, God's plan was to call all people as His own. But He first chose Israel to be His bride. And His bride needed to remain pure from anyone and anything that would tear her allegiance away from her Husband – because the Almighty's beloved Israel was to one day bear His perfect Son.

The entire history of God's chosen people, from Genesis to Malachi, reflected His protection and purification of them, so that He could one day fulfill His promise. Every single rule and every powerful redemption in the Old Testament had at its core the purpose of preserving the seed of Christ. And so, for a time, Israel had to remain set apart from the rest of mankind.

But with Jesus' birth, all the prophecies and promises of His lineage were fulfilled, and the dividing wall crumbled to the ground. The Magi were privileged to be the first Gentiles to hail the dawning of this new era. An era of global reconciliation and universal worship. Israel was blessed to birth the Messiah, but His mission was for every man, woman and child on the face of this earth, no matter their heritage, or their nationality, or their race. We are all heirs together, branches drawing life from the same vine.[46]

It is no longer of any consequence whether someone is a natural branch (a Jewish believer) or one that has been grafted in. Now we all – through faith in the True Vine, the Messiah[47] – can grow and mature together as one family, according to God's promise. In fact, the vine is even more beautiful than before, because it is full of countless kinds and colors of blooms growing together in a brilliant living bouquet.

Have you ever felt you couldn't come to Jesus because of your background? Have you ever decided that a person didn't look like someone who could love Jesus – or that He would love back? Open your heart to the truth that Jesus came for us all. Seek Him, no matter what your culture or your preconceived notions say to the contrary. And live for Him in a spirit of reconciliation and delight at the priceless tapestry He is weaving together through us all.

[The Magi] were divinely instructed...to [go to] their own country ...
Matthew 2:12b AMP

The first thing [Andrew] did after finding where Jesus lived was find his own brother, Simon, telling him, "We've found the Messiah" (that is, "Christ"). He immediately led him to Jesus.
John 1: 41 The Message

The woman then left her waterpot, went her way into the city, and said to the men, "Come and see a Man who told me all things that I ever did. Could this be the Christ?" Then they went out of the city and came to him. And many of the Samaritans of that city believed... "that this is indeed the Christ, the Savior of the world."
John 4:28-30,39,42 NKJV

...You're here to be light...God is not a secret to be kept...If I make you light-bearers, you don't think I'm going to hide you under a bucket, do you? ...shine! ...By opening up to others, you'll prompt people to open up with God, this generous Father in heaven."
Matthew 5:14-16 The Message

...His word is in my heart like a fire, a fire shut up in my bones.
I am weary of holding it in; indeed, I cannot.
Jeremiah 20:9 NIV

"...you shall be My witnesses...even to the remotest part of the earth."
Acts 1:8 NASB

Day Twenty Four
Let It Shine

The Magi's journey did not end in Bethlehem. Of course, their quest was to find the newborn Messiah in Judea and worship Him. But the final stop on their historic expedition was the very place where they began: home.

✸ Read the passages on the opposite page.

The Magi could have chosen to stay in the middle of their "mountaintop" experience. Forsaking their homeland to remain with Jesus would have demonstrated their faith. Protecting the holy family during their flight into Egypt would have confirmed the Magi's loyalty. And publicly establishing themselves as the first Gentile followers would have made clear the universal salvation offered by the Messiah. All good and godly options.

Except that staying on the mountaintop is not what the Magi were called to do. God Himself instructed them to take their encounter with Jesus back home, where the Magi's community must have been hungry for details about their long journey and their encounter with the rising Ruler from Jacob.

Decades later, the pattern continued. When Andrew first encountered Jesus, the first thing he did was go home and tell his brother. And after the infamous Samaritan woman encountered Jesus at the well, she marched straight back to the very people who had shunned her, and boldly shared her experience.

On the surface, these people were so different from one another. Royal astronomers. A blue collar fisherman. An immoral outcast. None of them had any formal Bible training. Only one was even Jewish. The only thing they had in common was a face-to-face encounter with Jesus. They were witnesses.

The Magi, Andrew, and the Samaritan woman simply bore witness to their personal encounters with Jesus. They didn't judge or defend or prosecute. They simply testified. Jesus has called us to do the same: to tell others about our experience with Him. So let us join with Peter, proclaiming that, "we cannot stop speaking of what we have seen and heard."[48]

What has Jesus done for you? Have you ever told anyone, or are you waiting until you are more "qualified?" No amount of training qualifies you to share about God more than your own personal experience. If you've never personally encountered the Savior, pray for Him to touch your life in a real way. And when He does, share it with anyone who will listen. Let it shine!

...[the Magi] went their way;
and the star, which they had seen in the east,
went on before them until it came and stood
over the place where the Child was.
When they saw the star, they
rejoiced exceedingly with great joy.
After coming into the house they saw the Child with Mary
His mother, and they fell to the ground and worshipped Him. Then,
opening their treasures, they presented to Him
gifts of gold, frankincense, and myrrh.

Matthew 2:9-11 NASB

I rejoice over Your promise
like one who finds vast treasure.

Psalm 119:162 HCSB

The people who walked in darkness have seen a great light...

Isaiah 9:1a ESV

You love Him, though you have not seen Him.
And though not seeing Him now, you believe in Him and rejoice with
inexpressible and glorious joy, because you are receiving the goal of your
faith, the salvation of your souls.

1 Peter 1:8-9 HCSB

Rejoice Exceedingly

Merry Christmas! This is the day we have been looking forward to all this time of Advent. It is the very same thing the Magi sought: to celebrate the birth of the Messiah. They had come so far for this very moment, to come face-to-face with the Promised One.

The Magi's journey to the Savior is like a beautifully wrapped gift to us on Christmas morning. It ties together everything about who Jesus is, everything He came to do all those years ago, and everything He longs to do in us today.

On this Christmas Day, let us ponder what is wrapped up in this priceless gift, recalling what the Magi's journey has revealed about the One we celebrate today: Jesus is the rising Star of Jacob. The Divine Scepter. The Everlasting King. The Great High Priest. The Perfect Sacrifice. The Light of the World. The Bread of Life. The Aroma of Healing. The True Vine. The Son of God.

✳ Read the passages on the opposite page.

The Magi's treasures of gold, frankincense, and myrrh paled in comparison to the gift they received in Bethlehem. A gift planned so perfectly, put together so intricately, and wrapped so delicately. Their immediate response was to rejoice. But not just to rejoice, to rejoice exceedingly with great joy!

The Greek tells us that the Magi's joyful greeting was exceedingly *megas* – the root of our word "mega." By definition, their outward rejoicing was abundant and mighty, loud and intense, massive and weighty, high and strong. Their joy burst forth like fireworks, the outward clamor evidence of the mega celebration within their hearts that they were simply unable to contain.

So today, when we greet others with "Merry Christmas," and when we sing together "Joy to the World," let us not simply be cheerful. Instead, let our voices rise outwardly and our hearts swell inwardly with abundant and mighty joy. Celebrate and worship as if you were one of the Magi, coming face-to-face with the long-awaited Messiah for the very first time.

As you celebrate today the birth of Jesus, the very Son of the Almighty God, I pray that you will rejoice exceedingly with great joy, and that you will determine to give Him the choicest gifts of your heart, your hands, and your worship. And that you would share Him abundantly with those around you.

Bibliography

Alexander, P. (1986). The Lion Encyclopedia of the Bible. Batania, IL: Lion Publishing Corporation.

Allen, C. J. (1969). The Broadman Bible Commentary, Volume 8: Matthew – Mark. Nashville, TN: Broadman Press.

Barclay, W., (1958). The Gospel of Matthew, Volume 1 (Second Edition). Philadelphia, PA: The Westminster Press.

Barnes, A. (1868). Notes on the New Testament: Matthew and Mark. Grand Rapids, MI: Baker Book House.

Blomberg, C. L. (1992). The New American Commentary Volume 22: Matthew. Nashville, TN: Broadman Press.

Butler, T. C. (1991). Holman Bible Dictionary. Nashville, TN: Holman Bible Publishers.

Cohen, A. (1949). Everyman's Talmud: The Major Teachings of the Rabbinic Sages. New York, NY: Schocken Books.

Davidiy, Y. (n.d.). Commentary on the Book of Micah. Retrieved from http://britam.org/micah.html.

Donley, J. (2006). The Everything History of the Bible Book: From Divine Inspiration to Modern Day Discoveries. Avon, MA: Adams Media.

Frankincense. (2011). In Encyclopaedia Brittanica Online. Retrieved from http://www.britannica.com/EBchecked/topic/217294/frankincense

Fritze, R. H. (2003). New Worlds: The Great Voyages of Discovery, 1400-1600. Westport, CT: Praeger Publishers.

Gildemeister, E. (1913). The Volatile Oils, Volume 1. New York, NY: John Wiley and Sons.

Henry, M. (1961). Matthew Henry's Commentary on the Whole Bible. Grand Rapids, MI: Zondervan.

Jamieson, R., Fausset, A. R., and Brown, D. (1871). "Commentary on Numbers 24." In Commentary Critical and Explanatory on the Whole Bible."

Kowalchik, C. Hylton, W. H. (1998). Rodale's Illustrated Encyclopedia of Herbs. Emmaus, PA: Rodale Books.

Lemenih, M. & Teketay, D. (2003). Frankincense and Myrrh Resources of Ethiopia. Ethiopian Journal of Science, 26(2),161-172.

MacArthur, J. (1978). Who Were the Wise Men? Retrieved from http://www.gty.org/Resources/Sermons/2182.

Margolis, M. L. (1908). The Holy Scriptures with Commentary: Micah. Philadelphia, PA: Jewish Publication Society of America.

Metzger, B. M. & Coogan, M. D. (1993). The Oxford Guide to the Bible. New York, NY: Oxford University Press.

Pentateuchal Targumim: Numbers 22-25 (n.d.). In *The International Organization for Targumic Studies*. Retrieved from http://targum.info/pj/pjnum22-25.htm.

Sarna, N. M. (1990). The JPS Torah Commentary: Numbers. New York, NY: The Jewish Publication Society.

Singer, I., Seligsohn, M., Gottheil, R. & Hirschfeld, H. (1901-1906). The Jewish Encyclopedia. Retrieved from http://www.jewishencyclopedia.com.

Stern, D. (1992). The Jewish New Testament Commentary. Clarksville, MD: Jewish New Testament Publications, Inc.

Stewart, D. (2003). Healing Oils of the Bible. Marble Hill, MO: Care Publications.

Vine, W. E. (1981). Vine's Expository Dictionary of Old and New Testament Words. Grand Rapids, MI: Fleming H. Revell Company.

Weber, S. K. (2000). Holman New Testament Commentary: Matthew. Nashville, TN: Broadman & Holman Publishers.

Wesley, J. (1754-1765). John Wesley's Explanatory Notes on the Whole Bible Retrieved from http://www.biblestudytools.com/Commentaries/WesleysExplanatoryNotes/.

Yemen. (2011). In Encyclopaedia Brittanica Online. Retrieved from http://www.britannica.com/EBchecked/topic/652831/Yemen.

Young, R. (1800). Robert Young's Analytical Concordance to the Holy Bible (12th printing of the 7th Edition). London: The Religious Tract Society.

Zodhiates, S. (1990). The Hebrew-Greek Key Study Bible (New American Standard). Chattanooga, TN: AMG Publishers.

Pronunciation Guide[*]

Adonai (ah-doe-*nigh*) (H) ....God with us

Adventus (ad-*ven*-tuss) (L) ....arrival, coming

Beit-Lechem (bait Leh-kehm) (H) ....Bethlehem, literally "house of bread"

Darak (dah-*rahk*) (H)...come out, or rise

Kohkav (koe-*kahv*) (H)..star (literally), prince (figuratively)

Loh (low) (H) ....to him

Maror (mah-*roar*) (H) ....bitter

Megas (meg-ahs) (G)...........................big, mighty, loud, heavy, massive, intense, exceedingly

Parousia (pah-roo-see-ah) (G)...presence, arrival

Shevet (sheh-*vet*) (H) ....scepter, rod, pointer, weapon or war, branch

Shai (shy) (H) ....tribute

Shellow (shell-*oh*) (H) ....that which belongs to him

Shiloh (shy-low) (H) ....*see Day Seven for a discussion of Shiloh's definition*

[*] G = Greek, H = Hebrew, L = Latin

Notes

1 Vine, W. E. (1981), p.208
2 Young, R. (1800), p.770
3 MacArthur, J. (1978) and Donley, J. (2006), among others.
4 Daniel 5:30
5 See Numbers 22 for the full story
6 Joshua 24
7 Nehemiah 13:2
8 Micah 6:5
9 2 Peter 2:15, Jude 1:11, and Revelation 2:14
10 Scripture accounts for more than 600,000 adult men (Exodus 1:5, Numbers 26:51), which most commentators expand to a total population of approximately two million.
11 See Joshua 1:3, Psalm 25:5,0, and Jeremiah 51:3a, 33, for example.
12 Fox, E. (1995), Sarna, N.M. (1990), and Wesley, J. (1754-1765)
13 See Psalm 45:6, Psalm 89:32, Isaiah 10:24, and Isaiah 14:5 for examples.
14 See Esther 5:2
15 Sarna, N.M. (1990), (p.178)
16 Sarna, N.M. (1990)
17 See, for example, 1 Samuel and Jeremiah 7:12
18 Sarna, N.M. (1990)
19 The Targum is an Aramaic translation of the Torah developed in Babylon and still read in conjunction with the Hebrew Scriptures today by very observant Jews.
20 Sarna, N.M. (1990)
21 1 Samuel 13:14
22 Jeremiah 29:11
23 Deuteronomy 4:19, 17:2-4
24 Henry, M. (1961)
25 Metzger & Coogan (1993)
26 Micah 5:2
27 Psalm 22:18
28 Zechariah 11:12-13
29 Fritze, R. H. (2003) and Yemen (2011)
30 Donley, J. (2006) and MacArthur, J. (1976), among others.
31 Psalm 24:10
32 Leviticus 17:11
33 Frankincense (2011) and Lenenih, M. & Teketay, D. (2003)
34 Frankincense (2011) and Lenenih, M. & Teketay, D. (2003)
35 Fritze, R. (2003) and Kowalchik, C. & Hylton, W. H. (1998)
36 Esther 2:12
37 Jamieson, Fausset & Brown (1871) and Stewart, D. (2003), among others
38 Exodus 25:8,22
39 Ruth 4:11
40 1 Samuel 17:12
41 Singer, I., Seligsohn, M., et. al. (1901-1906)
42 Davidiy, Y. (n.d.)
43 Zodiates, S. (1990)
44 Luke 2:25-38
45 Henry, M. (1961) among others.
46 See Romans 11 and John 15:1-8
47 John 15:1
48 Acts 4:20, NIV

About the Author

Tammy Priest grew up in a Jewish family where she learned the traditions of her faith. She embraced her heritage and became active in her local synagogue, continuing her involvement as a university student. Then one morning as she sang, God audibly spoke to the college senior with words she had never heard before: "Jesus is the Messiah."

Since that day, Tammy has been sharing the powerful testimony of her conversion. She also enjoys teaching adults, youth and children about the ways in which God's Old Testament and its rituals pointed perfectly to the coming Christ.

Tammy resides in Winston-Salem, North Carolina, with her husband, David, and their two children.

To learn more about Tammy's ministry and other publications, please visit her website (www.beginningwithmoses.net); send a letter to P.O. Box 25722, Winston-Salem, NC 27114-5722; or write an email to the ministry at info@beginningwithmoses.net.